I0797016

Chef Celeste's LOUISIANA KITCHEN

The Southern Table

Cynthia LeJeune Nobles, Series Editor

Chef Celeste's LOUISIANA KITCHEN

Simplifying Cajun & Creole Cuisine

CELESTE GILL

Louisiana State University Press   Baton Rouge

Published by Louisiana State University Press
lsupress.org

Copyright © 2025 by Celeste Gill
Foreword © 2025 by Louisiana State University Press
All rights reserved. Except in the case of brief quotations used in articles or reviews, no part of this publication may be reproduced or transmitted in any format or by any means without written permission of Louisiana State University Press.

Manufactured in Canada
First printing

Designer: Michelle A. Neustrom
Typefaces: Mokoko VF and Neulis Sans
Printer and binder: Friesens Corporation

Unless otherwise noted, all photographs are by Collin Richie.

Cataloging-in-Publication Data are available from the Library of Congress.
ISBN 978-0-8071-8497-4 (cloth: alk. paper)

Contents

3

Chicken 29

4

Seafood 43

Foreword

It is truly an honor and privilege to say a few words about Chef Celeste and her culinary world. Her mantra, "Good Food Is Homemade," is just the beginning of her life's journey in creating healthy and tasty meals.

Chef Celeste incorporates subtle changes in our classic Louisiana dishes by leaning on her unique life experiences that have brought her from Michigan to the Bayou State, with stops in Hawaii and Virginia. She has created her own special line of Certified Louisiana low-sodium seasonings, including an all-natural fat-free honey mustard, Creole garlic, cracked black pepper, and steak seasoning. They add delicious flavor and spice to all of her dishes, making every meal a culinary experience.

I first met Chef Celeste on her cooking show, *Cooking Up Louisiana Treasures,* where we showcased Louisiana specialty crops and connected them to local farmers and their stories. We cooked with the finest and freshest produce, meats, and fish available from local farmers' markets, roadside stands, and the local section of your favorite grocery store. We also enjoyed being together for cooking demonstrations at the Red Stick Farmers' Market on Main Street in downtown Baton Rouge.

With a twinkle in her eye, a great big smile, and unbridled passion, Chef Celeste brings to life delicious cuisine from simple local ingredients, all prepared with love and a flair for flavor. Try as she may, she still has a long way to go to train me as her sous-chef. I routinely reach for the wrong peppers, slice and dice green onions incorrectly, and am not quite sure exactly how much a pinch is. But the best part of cooking with Chef Celeste—either on *Cooking Up Louisiana Treasures* or on her other show, *My Louisiana Kitchen*—is not just being her designated sous-chef of the day but enjoying her mouthwatering creations right there on set when she is finished.

I am so happy that Chef Celeste has decided to publish this cookbook. Now you and I can look up the recipes and re-create her delicious, nutritious cuisine celebrating the rich culinary traditions of Louisiana.

Good Cooking,

Mike Strain
Commissioner
Louisiana Department of Agriculture and Forestry

Acknowledgments & Dedication

This cookbook is a tribute to my family. While my parents may not be here to read it, their unwavering support and encouragement were the driving force behind its creation.

A culinary heritage runs deep in my family, with numerous members having ventured into the restaurant industry. Although I call Baton Rouge my home, I grew up in Detroit, where my mom and grandmother both once graced the restaurant scene. These two remarkable women infused me with a profound appreciation for the culinary world. The echoes of their passion for cooking reverberate in each page of this cookbook.

My father was not much of a cook, but memories of our fishing escapades in scenic Canadian landscapes remain etched in my mind. Those idyllic times were some of the most treasured moments of my life. Our fishing trips were emblematic of the bond we shared and the lessons he taught me about the art of patience and connecting with nature.

Reflecting upon my life's journey, I am also grateful for the freedom and encouragement my family provided me, allowing me to evolve into the individual I am today. Their unyielding belief in my aspirations and their constant presence in my life have been the bedrock of my accomplishments.

Each recipe in this cookbook carries with it a piece of my family's legacy, a testament to their influence on my culinary endeavors. I extend my gratitude to all my family members who have played an integral role in shaping my path. From my parents who watch over me from above to those who continue to stand beside me, your love and support have been my guiding light. With utmost sincerity, I express my thanks and affection to each one of you.

Love y'all!

Chef Celeste's LOUISIANA KITCHEN

Introduction

Time to Smell the Roux

This cookbook tells the story of my journey to become Chef Celeste. My love of cooking started in the vibrant city of Detroit, my hometown. Over the years my culinary passion steered me to the lush landscapes of Hawaii, to Virginia, and, finally, to the soulful kitchens of Baton Rouge, Louisiana. In these pages you will discover how my diverse experiences have shaped me into the chef I am today. You will also learn that my career is the result of creating, nurturing, and celebrating the culinary aspirations that unite us all.

Over the years I have owned restaurants, cooked in institutional settings, and done too many cooking demonstrations to count. Aside from cooking professionally, I also like to teach. In each aspiring chef lies the potential to transform not just ingredients but also their own lives. For this reason I encourage my students to spark the flames of passion, purpose, and unwavering self-belief. I try to ignite not only culinary skills but also an unshakable determination to embrace their unique journey.

Through my teaching, I have been privileged to work with numerous individuals as they carve their own paths. Some have become dietary managers, caterers, and culinary entrepreneurs. One particular success story is a dishwasher who rose to the position of orchestrating dining experiences at private school venues. Another shining star is a former student now called Chef Priscilla. I have guided ten or so other outstanding chefs, mentees who have forged their paths in this at times daunting industry.

Since the principle "each one must teach one" is not merely a catchphrase for me, I often find myself teaching in diverse settings. One of my favorite teaching opportunities is in East Baton Rouge Parish school classrooms. And I would be remiss not to mention the rewarding things that go on in the kitchens of the East Baton Rouge Parish prison system, where I train inmates in culinary arts.

Teaching would-be chefs and prison inmates to cook is essentially the same. The primary difference lies in the students' incarceration status. Both groups begin with foundational food safety knowledge and progress through kitchen etiquette and basic culinary techniques. My experience in catering, particularly with the Baton Rouge Council on Aging, has reinforced the importance of ongoing on-the-job training, especially when preparing large-scale meals like the four thousand meals we serve daily.

No matter where I teach or cook, food, I've come to realize, is more than sustenance; it is a refuge for some and a therapy for others. Food possesses a remarkable ability to mend hearts, bridge distances, and bring people into harmonious communion. Through the simple act of preparing and sharing a meal, connections are forged, stories are exchanged, and bonds are woven. I've witnessed firsthand how a well-crafted dish can evoke nostalgia, create solace, and kindle joy.

Food can also shape destinies. It has gifted me the wings to travel, the courage to pursue dreams, and the joy of connecting with diverse cultures. Every plate I've prepared, every aroma I've conjured, has not just delighted palates but also served as a passport to explore the world and embrace my aspirations.

This is a very emotional and pivotal time in my life, and I've made important changes in order to devote time to my long-range goals. The fall of 2023 marked the end of my twenty years as the coordinator of cooking demonstrations inside the Main Street Market in downtown Baton Rouge. Although I will still do demos, the job of finding qualified and entertaining chefs has fallen to someone else. And recently I found someone to take over a job I have held at Southside Gardens Retirement

Community for seventeen years. I closed my Bistro at the NeuroMedical Center and my remaining restaurant, Chef Celeste Bistro in downtown Baton Rouge, in March 2024, the month of Easter, signaling a new birth for my career. Making these changes will allow me to grow in other areas. I've always had multiple dreams, and I have been fortunate to have some of those dreams fit into God's plan.

On this next journey, my focus is on teaching all things food through media. I have a show on the Eat This TV network, and I have my own national TV show called *My Louisiana Kitchen*. And I must mention that I am beginning the Chef Celeste Culinary Institute. I'm excited!

Aside from all that, I market seven "Senior Seasoning" blends. These low-sodium dry seasonings are the heart of everything that comes off my stove. I developed them out of necessity for the way I cook, for adding great flavor while keeping food low in sodium. (Don't worry, if you can't get your hands on my products, I'll give substitutions, and you can still make my recipes with fabulous results.)

Throughout my culinary journey, many dear friends and admirers have asked, "Why haven't you penned a cookbook yet?" I am crafting this cookbook as part of the long-range goals I mentioned earlier. I have juggled many endeavors for all of my culinary career. (This organized chaos may seem unmanageable to many, but to me it's normal.) Even so, I am aided in my work by a devoted and capable team. Since I do not feel burdened by my workload, I have taken the time to explore purpose and possibility, and writing a cookbook right now feels undeniably right. As with all significant undertakings, I've come to realize that one must be patient and wait for the opportune moment. In life, as in culinary creation, timing is everything.

Another driving force behind my decision to write this book was a few pages from Clay Morris's book *Inspired Cooking: A Collection of Short Stories and Recipes Shared*. Clay, a military veteran who fed many during the aftermaths of Hurricanes Katrina and Rita, is a dear friend of mine. He holds a special place in my heart. I had the honor of writing a foreword for his book, which encapsulates his culinary passion and spirit.

Two years ago, in the middle of my life's usual bustling chaos, Clay asked me to read page 54 of his book. At the time, I only had time to glance at it. But recently I concentrated on his words, and I uncovered something remarkable—a chronicle of Clay's visit to my restaurant Chef Celeste Bistro, which was nestled within Baton Rouge's vibrant Main Street Market.

In three pages, Clay recounted coming to my restaurant with his wife, Michelle, during a crucial period when they were looking for encouragement to write their own cookbook. As I read his words, I remembered a pivotal conversation we had then. My words to Clay were, "What are you waiting for?" Little did I realize that these words, meant to encourage my friend, would circle back to resonate deeply within me.

To Clay and Michelle, I extend my heartfelt appreciation for the unintentional role you've played in this chapter of my journey. Your words, your visit, and the mutual encouragement we exchanged have not only come full circle but have also ignited a renewed determination within me. It is a reminder that life's most profound lessons often come from the unlikeliest of sources, and the ripple effects of our actions can shape destinies in ways we may never fully anticipate.

So here I stand, at the intersection of experience and aspiration. With a heart brimming with enthusiasm and a clear path ahead, I am translating my culinary tales and expertise onto the pages of a cookbook.

The recipes in this book are easy to follow. I want to empower cooks of all levels to re-create in their own kitchens what I consider remarkable dishes. Whether you are a seasoned cook, a culinary enthusiast, or simply curious about the stories behind the dishes we Louisiana residents love, this cookbook promises an unforgettable voyage that combines flavors, traditions, and personal stories in every bite.

From my kitchen to yours, I offer these cherished recipes to you and your loved ones with heartfelt enthusiasm. Just as my family and I have relished the flavors and moments these dishes have brought, I sincerely hope that you, too, will find joy in every bite. I envision the laughter at gatherings, the warmth of shared meals, and the creation of lasting bonds as you embark on your own culinary adventures. May the aroma of these dishes fill your home with comfort and anticipation, and may the act of preparing them become a cherished ritual that brings your loved ones together. May these recipes serve as a constant reminder that the joy of cooking is not just in the delicious end result but also in the shared experiences and cherished memories that emerge along the way.

Things to Have on Hand

Basic Pantry Items

All-purpose flour
Black pepper
Cayenne pepper
Elbow macaroni
Frank's RedHot Sauce*
Fried chili oil
Garlic, granulated
Honey (local is best)
Honey mustard
Olive oil
Penne pasta
Potatoes, red
Rice, brown and white
Ro-Tel tomatoes
Salt
Spaghetti, thin
Spinach, canned
Steak seasoning
Sugar, granulated and dark brown
Tabasco sauce**
Tomato sauce
Vegetable oil

*Frank's RedHot Sauce is made in the Louisiana style. It is widely available and similar to Tabasco sauce, but with a hint of garlic that gives it a bit more complex flavor.

**Tabasco is the iconic, vinegar-based Louisiana-style hot sauce. It has a thin texture and a slightly salty taste. It is aged before bottling.

Refrigerator Items

Bell peppers (red and green)
Blue cheese
Butter
Celery
Cheddar cheese, shredded
Eggs
Garlic, whole in a jar
Lemon juice
Lemons
Limes
Milk
Parmesan cheese, shaved or wedge to grate as needed
Salad greens
Tomatoes

Freezer Items

Blueberries
Catfish fillets
Chicken, whole
Chuck roast
Crawfish tails
Ground beef, 80/20 fat ratio
Mango
Short Ribs
Shrimp, 31/35 or larger
Smoked sausage
Strawberries

Note: As a rule, I cook with fresh ingredients. But if you live in an area where this is challenging, by all means, load your freezer.

1

Soups

My culinary journey began in Detroit in the kitchen with my mom and my paternal grandmother, who at times lived with us. We had a family-style home-cooked meal every day, and I would join in on meal preparation. Various aunts and uncles often visited during the week, and food was often the center of the visits.

I was always curious about food. For example, I would ask my mom to buy a variety of "exotic" fruits, such as kiwi, passion fruit, and papaya. I certainly enjoyed eating these tropical goodies. I would also try them out on the family, most often receiving a thumbs-up.

I first was allowed to cook at the stove when I was around nine years old. My mom taught me the cuisine of her mother, which was southern cooking. Although my family lived in Detroit, we were still a product of the Great Migration from the South to the North. Therefore, we cooked smothered chicken and pork chops, rice and gravy, and a hearty chicken vegetable soup that you can find on page 15 of this cookbook.

In my childhood, I had nightmares of food chasing me. The monster might have been a giant tomato or banana. Maybe because of these dreams, I did not immediately go into the culinary field. Even though I liked to help cook, I did not think food preparation was my career path. Actually, I felt I was destined for anything except cooking. After high school, I became a licensed cosmetologist. For the next ten years, I styled hair and worked in an auto factory in Detroit, where I would cook for friends for their special events.

When I reflect on community expectations as I was growing up, I realize that our street in Detroit, Appoline, produced more than its share of above-average individuals. At twenty-one, my friend Vickie was the first to buy a home and dive into entrepreneurship with her lash salon. Another neighbor became a fashion designer with her own studio. The street was home to countless future veterans of the US Armed Forces, restaurant owners, and actors. We grew up three doors from Courtney B. Vance, the husband of actress Angela Bassett and an actor in his own right. It was an unspoken expectation in our home that we do our best. Although my parents are no longer here, they know . . . I'm doing my best.

Shrimp and Corn Soup

Makes 6 servings

2 tablespoons vegetable oil or butter
1 cup freshly cut corn off the cob
¼ cup chopped celery
2 tablespoons chopped yellow onion
2 tablespoons chopped green bell pepper
2 tablespoons chopped green onion
2 tablespoons roasted garlic
4 cups heavy cream
1 pound shrimp, cleaned and chopped
2 tablespoons all-purpose flour or 1 teaspoon cornstarch
¼ cup shrimp stock
½ pound whole 31/35 shrimp, cleaned
1 teaspoon black pepper
¼ teaspoon salt
⅛ teaspoon cayenne pepper
For serving: crackers

1. Heat oil in a stockpot set over medium-high heat. Add corn, celery, onion, bell pepper, green onion, and garlic and cook until everything is tender, about 7 minutes.

2. Stir in cream and chopped shrimp and cook on medium heat 20 minutes, stirring constantly.

3. Thoroughly whisk together the flour and shrimp stock, then whisk into the soup. Add the ½ pound whole shrimp. Cook an additional 10 minutes.

4. Add seasonings and cook an additional 5 minutes. Serve hot with crackers.

Tip: Cooked diced potatoes make a nice addition to this soup. You can also use this soup to top pasta or a baked potato.

Tomato Basil Soup

Makes 8 servings

5 large tomatoes, preferably locally grown
3 cups vegetable broth
¼ cup olive oil
1 large yellow onion, medium diced
1 yellow bell pepper, medium diced
4 cloves garlic, minced
6 leaves fresh basil
Salt and paper to taste
1 cup heavy cream
For serving: croutons

1. Preheat oven to 400°F. Cut the tomatoes in half, place them on a baking sheet, and roast them until slightly golden, about 15 minutes.

2. In a large saucepan, combine roasted tomatoes, broth, olive oil, onion, bell pepper, garlic, basil, salt, and pepper. Simmer until vegetables are tender, about 45 minutes.

3. Cool the mixture, then blend until smooth. (It is important not to blend the mixture while it is hot; it may explode, causing injury.) Add heavy cream and blend well. Over medium heat, heat soup thoroughly, but do not let it boil. (135° degrees is ideal.) Adjust the salt and pepper to taste.

4. Pour into serving bowls and garnish with croutons.

Hearty Chicken Vegetable Soup

Makes 8 servings

- 1 whole chicken, roasted
- ¼ cup olive oil
- 3 large Idaho potatoes, peeled and diced
- 3 beefsteak tomatoes, unseeded and diced
- 1 large onion, diced
- 1 large bell pepper, medium diced
- 1 medium carrot, medium diced
- 1 large clove garlic, minced
- 1 cup frozen green peas
- 1 cup cut green beans
- ½ gallon vegetable broth
- 1 tablespoon curry powder
- 1 teaspoon cayenne pepper, or to taste
- 1 teaspoon black pepper
- Salt to taste

1. Debone the roasted chicken. Discard the bones and set the meat aside.
2. Add oil, potatoes, tomatoes, onion, bell pepper, carrot, garlic, peas, and green beans to a large stockpot. Cook until vegetables are browned, about 15 minutes. Add broth and bring to a gentle boil. Cook 15 more minutes.
3. Add the reserved chicken, curry powder, cayenne, black pepper, and salt and simmer 30 minutes. Adjust seasonings and serve hot.

Black Bean Soup

Makes 6 servings

2 tablespoons olive oil
½ large onion, diced
¼ cup diced carrots
4 cloves garlic, minced
2 (12-ounce) cans black beans
⅓ cup tomato paste
1 cup chicken stock
1 bay leaf
1 teaspoon salt
½ teaspoon ground sage
½ teaspoon white pepper
½ teaspoon cumin
For serving: shredded Cheddar cheese, chopped cilantro, and sour cream

1. Add olive oil to a large pot set over low heat. Add onion, carrots, and garlic. Cook until onion is translucent, about 8 minutes. Add black beans and tomato paste. Cook 10 minutes.
2. Add chicken stock, bay leaf, and seasonings. Simmer on low heat 30 minutes. Serve hot in bowls and garnish with cheese, cilantro, and sour cream.

Lentil Soup

Makes 6 servings

1 tablespoon butter or ghee
½ cup mirepoix*
2 cups dry lentils
2 cloves garlic, minced
2 cups beef or vegetable stock
1 teaspoon curry powder
1 teaspoon salt
½ teaspoon black pepper
½ cup water, if necessary

1. In a large pot set over medium heat, melt butter and add mirepoix. Sauté 5 minutes, then reduce heat to low. Add lentils and cook 5 minutes. (Cooking lentils without much moisture toasts them and adds depth to the soup.) Add garlic and sauté 30 seconds.
2. Add stock, curry powder, salt, and pepper and simmer 30 minutes.
3. Puree half of the soup until smooth. Add pureed soup back to the pot. Thin with water if necessary. Simmer an additional 15 minutes and serve hot.

* Mirepoix is a mixture of an equal amount of diced onion, bell pepper, celery, and carrots. The traditional Louisiana style, which can be found in grocery freezer or produce sections, usually does not contain carrots.

Potato and Leek Soup

Makes 4 servings

3 large leeks
1 tablespoon butter
2-inch link smoked sausage, diced
½ large onion, diced
3 medium Idaho potatoes, boiled and cubed
1 cup milk
1 tablespoon grated Parmesan cheese
2 teaspoons salt
1 teaspoon black pepper
1 teaspoon garlic powder
1 tablespoon chives, minced
1 cup water, if necessary
For serving: sour cream and chopped chives

1. Rinse the leeks thoroughly, removing all traces of sand. Cut off the dark-green tops and discard. Cut the remainder into half-moons.
2. In a large pot set over medium heat, melt butter and add leeks, sausage, and onion. Cook until leeks are soft and onion is transparent, about 5 minutes.
3. Add potatoes and milk. Mash the potatoes and bring the mixture to a simmer over low heat. Cook 10 minutes. Add Parmesan, salt, pepper, and garlic powder. If soup is too thick, add up to 1 cup water. Bring to a simmer and cook 10 more minutes.
4. For a smooth soup, blend on low speed in batches 30 seconds at a time. Serve hot in bowls and top with sour cream and chives.

2

Salads

My mother and grandmother were my family's main cooks. I was the sole helper. My three siblings had other interests and did not partake in the cooking rituals.

I call my family's meal preparation a ritual because in many households the cooking process reflects heritage and tradition. For many women, cooking is also a rite of passage. The hours spent together in the kitchen is a time for bonding and learning life's lessons. Think of the stories you were told or overheard in your family's kitchen.

With help from my mother and grandmother, I started my cooking journey by making potato salad. When I was only four years old, I loved to help peel the cooked potatoes. That potato salad recipe is still one of our family favorites.

Potatoes and pasta are two of my top indulgences. There's something about the creamy texture of a perfectly cooked potato that I crave. I know that a fried potato is cooked when the flesh is easy to mash with your teeth, or with a fork if you want to mash potatoes. Perfect pasta is the opposite of a perfect potato. Pasta should be soft but firm to the bite. Not hard, not mushy, but with just that right amount of give.

I've included a pasta and a potato recipe in this chapter. You'll also find a recipe for sautéed shrimp salad, which launched my product line. Sautéed shrimp was a popular dish in my restaurant. To have consistency, I created the recipe for the sauce, which I now sell bottled.

Sautéed Shrimp Salad

Makes 4 servings

Fortunately, it is easy to find fresh Gulf shrimp in South Louisiana. To me, freshness is essential for the success of this recipe.

¼ cup olive oil
2 pounds fresh, large Louisiana shrimp, peeled and deveined
4 garlic cloves, minced
1 cup Chef Celeste's Honey Mustard, or ½ cup each mustard and honey and 1 tablespoon black strap molasses
3 tomatoes, wedged
1 small head cabbage, shredded
1 bunch kale, shredded
1 fennel bulb, sliced
2 tablespoons Cajun seasoning
1 tablespoon Chef Celeste's Creole Garlic Seasoning, or equal parts Italian seasoning, paprika, and onion powder
1 teaspoon fish sauce
Salt and pepper to taste
For serving: crisp salad greens

1. In a large skillet set over medium-high heat, heat olive oil and sauté shrimp and garlic until the shrimp turns bright pink, about 10 minutes.
2. Add Honey Mustard and all other ingredients. Cook an additional 2 minutes. Pour over salad greens and serve immediately.

Pasta Salad

Makes 4 servings

Feel free to add things like salami, diced onion, or whatever your heart desires.

3 cups cooked orzo or rotini pasta
½ cup olive mix
½ cup grated Parmesan cheese
½ cup diced tomatoes
3 tablespoons olive oil
3 tablespoons Chef Celeste's Honey Mustard, or 1½ tablespoons each honey and mustard
2 tablespoons minced garlic
¼ teaspoon salt
¼ teaspoon black pepper

Combine all ingredients and chill. (Also delicious served hot.)

Potato Salad

Makes 6 servings

To make macaroni salad, substitute elbow macaroni for potatoes. Good additions are canned tuna, fresh chopped bell pepper, and onions.

3 large red potatoes, peeled and diced
1 cup mayonnaise
1 boiled egg, chopped (optional)
¼ cup pickle relish
3 tablespoons yellow mustard
2 tablespoons sugar
1 teaspoon salt
1 teaspoon black pepper

Boil and cool potatoes. Combine cooled potatoes with all ingredients and chill.

Chicken Salad

Makes 6 servings

This recipe is so simple, but everyone loves it! It was the top-selling sandwich in my restaurants. You can add onion, celery, and eggs to this versatile recipe. You can also replace the chicken with tuna.

- 1 pound chicken breasts, poached
- ¾ cup mayonnaise
- ¼ cup Chef Celeste's Honey Mustard, or 2 tablespoons each honey and mustard
- 2 teaspoons chopped parsley
- 2 teaspoons garlic powder
- 2 teaspoons Chef Celeste's Creole Garlic Seasoning, or equal parts Italian seasoning, paprika, and onion powder
- 1 teaspoon salt
- 1 teaspoon pepper
- 1 teaspoon paprika

Chop chicken finely. Combine with all other ingredients and chill.

Garden Salad with Italian Vinaigrette Dressing

Makes 6 servings

1 head green leaf lettuce, sliced
½ red onion, sliced
1 small cucumber, sliced
2 tomatoes, wedged
¼ cup shredded carrots
3 boiled eggs
1 teaspoon blue cheese or your favorite cheese
For serving: Italian Vinaigrette Dressing (recipe follows)

Arrange the lettuce slices in the center of a serving platter. Place mounds of onion slices, cucumbers, and tomatoes on the sides of the lettuce. Place shredded carrots in the center of the lettuce. Cut the eggs in half and place around the carrots. Sprinkle with cheese and top with dressing. Serve immediately.

Tip: You can add croutons and omit cheese and eggs. Chicken, shrimp, or tuna would also be delicious additions.

Italian Vinaigrette Dressing

Makes 1½ cups

1 cup vinegar
½ cup olive oil
1 tablespoon grated Parmesan cheese (optional)
¼ teaspoon dried basil
¼ teaspoon dried oregano
Salt, black pepper, and sugar to taste

Add everything to a covered glass jar and shake well. Serve immediately.

Shrimp Salad with Honey Mustard Vinaigrette

Makes 6 servings

- 1 pound jumbo shrimp, peeled and deveined
- 2 cloves garlic, minced
- ¼ teaspoon paprika
- Salt to taste
- 1 teaspoon olive oil
- 2 tablespoons Chef Celeste's Honey Mustard, or 1 tablespoon each honey and mustard
- ½ teaspoon red pepper flakes
- Black pepper to taste
- 2 cups spring-mix lettuce
- 1 cup fresh spinach
- For serving: Honey Mustard Vinaigrette (recipe follows)

1. Mix shrimp with garlic, paprika, and salt and set aside.
2. Heat oil in a skillet set over medium heat. Add seasoned shrimp and sauté 4 minutes. Add Honey Mustard, red pepper flakes, and black pepper. Cook an additional 2 minutes.
3. Combine spring mix and spinach and divide among 6 plates. Top with Honey Mustard Vinaigrette, and then warm shrimp. Serve immediately.

Honey Mustard Vinaigrette

Makes 2½ cups

- 1 cup olive oil
- 1 cup apple cider vinegar
- ¼ cup minced red onion
- 2 cloves minced garlic
- 1 tablespoon Dijon mustard
- 1 tablespoon honey
- ¼ teaspoon salt
- ¼ teaspoon cracked black pepper

Combine all ingredients. At room temperature, use within 4 hours. Store in the refrigerator up to 2 days.

Sensation Salad

Makes 4 servings

Before Jake Staples opened his own Baton Rouge restaurant (The Place), he and his brother Bob owned Bob & Jake's, an upscale steakhouse. From that eatery came a most famous culinary creation, the Sensation Salad. Introduced in the 1950s, the salad's fame spread when it was featured in the first edition of the Junior League of Baton Rouge's *River Road Recipes* in 1959. The salad's dressing is a basic vinaigrette, but it becomes so much more with the addition of grated Romano and fresh lemon juice. The tangy Sensation Salad Dressing pairs so well with all the salad components. Another thing to note is that this recipe calls for fresh lemon juice. This is very important.

- ½ cup vegetable oil
- ¼ cup fresh chopped parsley
- ¼ cup grated Romano cheese
- 2 garlic cloves, minced
- ¼ cup freshly squeezed lemon juice
- 1 tablespoon salt
- 1 tablespoon sugar
- 1 tablespoon Creole mustard
- 1 tablespoon mayonnaise
- 1 large head romaine lettuce
- For serving: croutons and grated Parmesan cheese

Mix everything together except the lettuce and refrigerate. When ready to serve, chop the lettuce, pour the dressing on top, and sprinkle with croutons and grated Parmesan.

Tip: This dressing makes a great sandwich topping.

3

Chicken

Chicken has universal appeal. Whether you're a seasoned home cook or a novice in the kitchen, chicken offers a friendly starting point for culinary exploration. Its mild flavor serves as a blank slate, ready to absorb the rich tapestry of tastes and aromas that define cuisines from around the globe.

The recipes in this chapter cater to a spectrum of preferences and occasions. From comforting classics that evoke nostalgia to innovative dishes that creatively push the boundaries, this section is a treasure trove of chicken-centric inspiration.

The recipe most dear to my heart is for my grandmother's fried chicken. Her chicken was more than a dish; it was a gateway to a time long past. In her kitchen, I discovered the warmth of tradition and the secret language of love. Her fried chicken, a crispy perfection bathed in a blend of spices known only to her, held the whispers of family history.

As a child, I would sit at the kitchen table, my eyes wide with anticipation, watching Grandma work her fried chicken magic. As she expertly lowered the chicken into bubbling hot oil, the kitchen would fill with the crisp melody of frying. The golden-brown chicken would dance in the hot oil, releasing a fragrance that seemed to hug every corner of the room. Impatiently we waited, our stomachs rumbling in harmony with the sizzling oil.

Finally, the moment of truth would arrive. Grandma would carefully lift the golden-brown treasure from the oil and place it on a waiting platter lined with paper towels. The chicken glistened with a sheen, each piece a masterpiece of crispy perfection. We would excitedly gather around the table, eyes fixed on the mouthwatering platter before us.

My grandmother's culinary alchemy wasn't just about frying chicken; it was a legacy, a tangible link to the past that made every meal a timeless celebration. In her kitchen, love had a flavor, and it was golden.

Not everyone who grew up in our household of cooks caught on to cooking. My older sister Sherrill is the only person I know who fried chicken in ten minutes. It was golden brown on the outside and, you guessed it, raw inside. She has since become a much better cook. Myself, I love the flexibility of poultry; it can be as complex as Coq Au Vin, as simple as grilled chicken, or anywhere in between.

Coq Au Vin

Makes 4 servings (begin a day ahead)

1 chicken, cut in 8 pieces
Creole seasoning or salt and pepper
2 cups sliced mushrooms
2 carrots, sliced thin
1 medium onion, chopped
1 stalk celery, chopped medium
2 cloves garlic, chopped
2 bay leaves
2 bunches parsley, chopped
2 pinches basil
1 pinch oregano
1 tablespoon cracked black pepper
10 ounces dry red wine
10 ounces chicken stock
¼ pound bacon
½ cup olive oil
2 tablespoons all-purpose flour
For serving: hot cooked noodles

1. The day before, place chicken pieces in a deep pan (not aluminum) and sprinkle with Creole seasoning. Add mushrooms, carrots, onion, celery, garlic, bay leaves, parsley, basil, oregano, and black pepper. Add wine and stock. Cover and refrigerate overnight.

2. The next day, remove carrots and discard. Remove the mushrooms and set aside. Remove the chicken and strain the onions and remaining vegetables from the liquid, retaining both. Cut bacon in small pieces and render it in the olive oil in a skillet over medium-high heat. Retaining the oil in the skillet, remove the bacon and set aside.

3. Sauté the marinated chicken in the oil and bacon grease. When chicken is a nice brown color, remove from the pan and set aside.

4. In the same pan, reduce the fire to medium low and add the reserved onion mixture. Cover and cook until tender, about 10 minutes. Add flour and mix well. Add the reserved liquid and stir until bubbly and thick. Add the chicken and bacon.

5. Stir and bring to a boil. Reduce heat and cook, covered, until chicken is very tender, about 1 hour. Stir gently every 10 minutes. About 30 minutes before it's cooked, add the mushrooms. Taste stew for seasoning. Serve hot over noodles.

Bourbon Roasted Chicken

Makes 4 servings

This is a crowd-pleaser, as well as a family meal. Since the alcohol burns off in the cooking process, I did not mind serving it to my children. For a one-pot meal, I cut the chicken into chunks before baking and mix it and the vegetables with cooked rice.

1 pound boneless chicken pieces
1 cup olive oil
4 cloves garlic, minced
3 tablespoons Chef Celeste's Creole Garlic Seasoning, or equal parts Italian seasoning, paprika, and onion powder
1 tablespoon cracked black pepper
2 teaspoons salt
¼ teaspoon cayenne pepper
1 cup bourbon or 1 cup orange juice
1 medium onion, diced
1 bell pepper, diced
2 tablespoons fresh grated ginger

1. Cut chicken into large serving pieces. In a small bowl, combine olive oil, garlic, Creole Garlic Seasoning, black pepper, salt, and cayenne. Rub mixture into chicken all over. Cover chicken and marinate overnight in the refrigerator.

2. Preheat oven to 375°F. To a large covered pot or roaster, add the chicken and marinade, the bourbon, onion, bell pepper, and ginger. Bake, covered, for 35 minutes. Uncover and bake until chicken reaches a minimum internal temperature of 165°F, about 30 more minutes. Serve warm.

Tip: This recipe can be made with a whole chicken, Cornish hens, or pork. You can also add chili pepper flakes and oil. Make this versatile recipe your own—change it up however you'd like.

Pan-Seared Honey-Lime Chicken

Makes 4 servings

8 chicken breast tenders
1 teaspoon salt
1 teaspoon cracked black pepper
¼ cup olive oil
¼ chopped green onion
2 cloves garlic, minced
1 lime, juiced
3 tablespoons Celeste's Honey Mustard, or 1½ tablespoons each honey and mustard
1 tablespoon freshly minced ginger

1. Season chicken with salt and pepper. Heat oil in a saucepan set over medium-high heat. Add chicken and brown on all sides.
2. Add remaining ingredients and sauté until chicken is thoroughly cooked, about 6 minutes. Serve warm.

Tip: Serve with Garlic-Herb Lima Beans (recipe page 78) and a salad.

Chicken and Sausage Jambalaya

Makes 10 servings

Every Louisiana cook worth her salt knows how to make jambalaya. I make mine the Cajun way, without tomato, as opposed to the New Orleans Creole version, which has lots of tomato.

2 pounds uncooked long-grain rice
½ cup vegetable oil
1 pound boneless chicken
1 pound smoked pork sausage, sliced
¼ cup chopped onion
¼ cup chopped bell pepper
2 cups chicken stock
2 cups beef stock
2 cups water
¼ cup chopped garlic
¼ cup chopped parsley
2 tablespoons granulated garlic
1 tablespoon paprika
1 teaspoon salt
1 teaspoon black pepper
⅛ teaspoon cayenne pepper

1. In a large Dutch oven set over medium heat, brown rice in oil 10 minutes, stirring often (This helps achieve the proper color.) Add chicken, sausage, onion, and bell pepper and sauté an additional 10 minutes.

2. Add the remaining ingredients. Cover and simmer over low heat until the liquid has absorbed, and the rice is tender, about 40 minutes. Remove from heat and let sit, covered, at least 5 minutes. Fluff rice and serve warm.

Tip: Some folks like to add pulled pork to jambalaya. Traditionally, jambalaya is served with white beans.

Fried Chicken

Makes 4 servings

This recipe is a fond memory of my grandmother's fried chicken. I give it a Cajun/Creole touch through the seasoning.

- 3-pound chicken, cut into 8 pieces
- 2 tablespoons Cajun or Creole seasoning
- 1 tablespoon paprika
- 1 tablespoon onion powder
- 1 tablespoon granulated garlic powder
- 1 quart buttermilk
- 2½ cups all-purpose flour
- 1 quart cooking oil, for frying

1. Remove excess fat from chicken and place the chicken into a bowl. In a small bowl, mix the Cajun seasoning, paprika, onion powder, and garlic powder. Sprinkle half the spice mixture on the chicken and rub into the meat evenly. Pour the buttermilk over the chicken. Cover and refrigerate at least 4 hours or up to overnight.
2. Pour the flour and remaining spice mixture into a bag, bowl, or dish. Remove the chicken from the buttermilk and shake off the excess liquid. Add the chicken pieces to the flour mixture and shake or dredge until chicken is well coated. Set aside.
3. Heat oil in a deep fryer or frying pan to 350°F. Carefully place the chicken pieces into the oil. Do not overcrowd the pan. It is okay to fry in batches. Turn the chicken as it browns. Larger parts such as breast, thighs, and legs take 12–16 minutes, while wings take about 8–10 minutes.
4. Drain the cooked chicken on paper towels or a wire rack. Let sit 5–10 minutes before serving.

Oven-Roasted Chicken

Makes 4 servings

1 (4- to 5-pound) whole chicken
5 tablespoons softened butter
2 tablespoons dried rosemary
2 teaspoons seasoned salt
1½ teaspoons paprika
1 teaspoon garlic powder
1 teaspoon dried oregano
¾ teaspoon black pepper
½ teaspoon chili powder
½ teaspoon salt
2 tablespoons minced garlic
1 teaspoon lemon juice
1 tablespoon chopped parsley
For serving: Fresh rosemary for garnish

1. Preheat oven to 425°F. Rinse the inside of the chicken and use a paper towel to pat the skin dry.

2. In a bowl stir together the softened butter, dried rosemary, seasoned salt, paprika, garlic powder, oregano, black pepper, chili powder, and salt. Use your hands to smear the butter mixture all over the skin of the chicken.

3. Place the chicken in a shallow baking pan and bake until a meat thermometer inserted into the thickest part of the breast registers 160° F, about 40 minutes. About halfway through cooking, spoon some of the liquid from the bottom of the pan over the top of the chicken and into the chicken cavity.

4. Remove the chicken from the oven and pour all the liquid into a small saucepan. Cover the chicken with foil and set aside. Place the saucepan of liquid over high heat and add the minced garlic. Bring to a boil, then lower to a gentle simmer and cook until reduced by half, 5–7 minutes. Stir in the lemon juice and parsley.

5. To serve, carve the chicken, place the pieces on a platter, and spoon the sauce on top. Garnish with fresh rosemary.

Chicken Florentine

Makes 4 servings

- 3–4 boneless, skinless chicken breasts
- 1 egg, beaten
- 1 cup breadcrumbs (Italian style or plain or a mixture)
- ½ cup grated Parmesan cheese
- 3 tablespoons olive oil
- 3 tablespoons butter, divided
- ¼ cup minced onion
- 1 clove garlic, minced
- 2 (10-ounce) packages frozen chopped spinach, thawed and drained
- 2 tablespoons all-purpose flour
- ½ cup white wine
- 2 cups whole milk
- 2 tablespoons grated Swiss cheese
- 2 tablespoons grated Parmesan cheese
- Dash grated nutmeg
- For serving: hot pasta or rice

1. Preheat oven to 350°F. Cut chicken breasts in half and pound to ½-inch thick. Place egg in a shallow bowl. Combine breadcrumbs and Parmesan cheese and spread out on a plate. Heat oil in a heavy skillet over medium heat. Dip chicken pieces in egg and coat both sides with the breadcrumb mixture. Cook chicken pieces until golden brown, about 3 minutes each side. Place on paper towels to drain.

2. Melt 1 tablespoon butter in a skillet and sauté onion and garlic until onion is translucent, about 3 minutes. Add spinach. Cook until combined and heated through. Oil a 9×13-inch baking pan and spread spinach mixture on the bottom of the pan.

3. To make a cream sauce, make a light roux by combining the remaining 2 tablespoons butter and the flour in a medium saucepan. Cook over medium heat, stirring constantly, for 1 minute. Increase the heat to medium-high, add the wine, and whisk until smooth. Whisking constantly, slowly add the milk. Add the Swiss and Parmesan cheeses and the nutmeg and cook until thick and creamy.

4. Pour half the sauce over the spinach. Place chicken pieces on top, then top with the remaining sauce. Place the pan in the oven and cook until bubbly, about 30 minutes. Serve warm with pasta or rice.

Curry Chicken

Makes 6 servings

- 3 tablespoons olive oil
- 1 small onion, chopped
- 2 cloves garlic, minced
- 1 bay leaf
- 3 tablespoons curry powder
- 1 teaspoon ground cinnamon
- 1 teaspoon paprika
- ½ teaspoon grated fresh ginger root
- ½ teaspoon white sugar
- Salt to taste
- 2 skinless, boneless chicken breast halves, cut into bite-size pieces
- 1 cup plain yogurt
- ¾ cup coconut milk
- 1 tablespoon tomato paste
- ½ lemon, juiced
- ½ teaspoon cayenne pepper
- For serving: hot cooked rice

1. Heat olive oil in a skillet over medium heat. Sauté onion until lightly browned, about 5 minutes. Stir in garlic, bay leaf, curry powder, cinnamon, paprika, ginger root, sugar, and salt. Continue stirring for 2 minutes.
2. Add chicken pieces, yogurt, coconut milk, and tomato paste. Bring to a boil, reduce heat, and simmer 20–25 minutes.
3. Remove bay leaf and stir in lemon juice and cayenne pepper. Simmer 5 more minutes. Serve hot as it is or over rice.

Chicken Pot Pie

Makes 6 servings

2 medium-large chicken breasts, cut into 1-inch pieces
Salt and pepper, to taste
4 tablespoons (½ stick) butter, plus extra for the dish
1 white or yellow onion, diced
4 whole carrots, peeled and diced
2 celery stalks, chopped
1 tablespoon fresh thyme leaves
3 tablespoons all-purpose flour
1 cup chicken broth
1½ cups half-and-half or whole milk
¾ cup frozen peas
2 sheets refrigerated pie crust, or one homemade double pie crust
1 egg, lightly beaten

1. Preheat oven to 425°F. Season chicken well with salt and pepper and set aside. Melt the butter in a large skillet, Dutch oven, or frying pan set over medium-high heat. Stir in the onion, carrot, and celery, along with a pinch of salt. Cook until the onion is soft and starting to color, about 6 minutes.

2. Stir in the thyme, followed by the chicken. Cook until the chicken starts to brown. Sprinkle with the flour and stir and cook 1 minute. Pour in the broth and the half-and-half. Cook, stirring often, until the sauce thickens slightly but is a little thinner than you want the finished pie filling.

3. Stir in frozen peas, then remove from the heat. Add a little more salt and pepper, if needed, and set aside to cool a little.

4. While the filling cools, lightly butter a 9-inch pie plate and line it with one of the pie crusts.

5. Add the filling to the lined pie plate and brush the exposed pastry edges with beaten egg. Lay the other pie crust on top and press down to seal the edges. Trim off any excess with a sharp knife and crimp the edges.

6. Brush the top of the pie crust with egg and cut a small slit in the middle to let out steam. Bake until the pastry is cooked and the top is golden, 30–35 minutes. Let the pie to rest 10–15 minutes before slicing.

BBQ Chicken

Makes 4–6 servings

2 tablespoons brown sugar
2 large cloves garlic, chopped
2 teaspoons salt
1 teaspoon black pepper
10 pieces chicken
2 tablespoons vegetable oil
½ cup finely chopped onion
¾ cup ketchup
2 tablespoons white wine vinegar
2 tablespoons Worcestershire sauce

1. In a small bowl, blend brown sugar, garlic, salt, and pepper to form a paste. Spoon paste into a resealable plastic bag large enough to hold the chicken. Add the chicken and coat it with the paste. Squeeze out excess air and seal the bag. Marinate in the refrigerator at least 1 hour or up to overnight.

2. When ready to cook, heat oil in a small saucepan over medium heat. Add onion and sauté until softened, about 5 minutes. Stir in ketchup, vinegar, and Worcestershire sauce. Bring to a simmer and cook until flavors blend, about 10 minutes.

3. Heat a charcoal, pellet, or your favorite method grill to 375°F. Wrap the chicken in foil and grill 20 minutes, turning once halfway through.

4. Remove the foil, then return chicken to the grill. Baste lightly with sauce, then continue to cook, basting every 10 minutes, until chicken is no longer pink at the bone and the juices run clear, 20–25 more minutes. A thermometer inserted near the bone should read at least 165°F. Remove from heat and let sit at least 10 minutes before serving.

4

Seafood

Although I loved working in my mother's kitchen, I also loved salmon fishing in Canada with my dad. The Detroit River is only five miles away from my childhood home. The two of us would set out before dawn with our rods and reels and an ice chest with sandwiches. We'd stay for hours. When we arrived home, my father would clean and fillet our catch, and my grandmother would enjoy a bowl of milk and fresh salmon roe.

Shrimp has always been another favorite seafood, and one of my favorite shrimp dishes is Shrimp and Grits. In my restaurant I made things easy by seasoning the dish with my very own Senior Seasoning Creole Garlic blend. This dry seasoning is a mixture of all the herbs and spices necessary for my succulent shrimp sauce. (I decided to put everything in a jar so that, literally, all you need is shrimp, water, my Creole Garlic Seasoning, and flour, and you're done!) But don't worry—if you can't get your hands on my seasoning mix, you can substitute any dry Creole seasoning. Look for one with paprika, garlic, black pepper, parsley, onion, basil, oregano, savory, marjoram, rosemary, and a hint of salt.

When it comes to seafood, I guess I'm doing something right, because a few years ago I won the "Seafood Award" from Baton Rouge's Capital Chefs' Showcase contest. For other recipes, I have won accolades as "Chef of the Year" from the American Culinary Federation and first place in Baton Rouge's Fall Heat Cooking Competition. Because these events led to so many requests for spices and seasonings, I began packaging and selling my own Louisiana Honey Mustard and proprietary Senior Seasoning spice blends, which have limited salt.

Excess dietary salt is a concern for the elderly, and I and my expanding team have always had our finger on the pulse of healthy senior dining by using the minimum amount of salt. My team provides meals for the East Baton Rouge Parish Council on Aging, daily serving twenty-two Senior Centers/Nutritional Feeding Sites with 1,100 hot meals, as well as 1,800 daily Meals on Wheels. During my seventeen years with the Southside Gardens Retirement Center, I served meals to independent as well as assisted living residents, some with special diet requirements. I also worked with the Spine Hospital of Louisiana, which ranks in the top 5 percent of hospitals in the country for its dietary considerations.

My seasonings also appear at my newest venture, which is a refurbished house in downtown Baton Rouge. I use the building's street address, 520 Spain Street, as its name, and it is a beautiful venue where clients host parties and events.

Shrimp and Grits

Makes 6 servings

This recipe was the inspiration for the creation of my dry, low-salt Senior Seasonings spice blends.

Grits

4 cups water
1 teaspoon salt
1 cup yellow stone-ground grits
1 cup shredded yellow Cheddar cheese
1 teaspoon coarsely ground black pepper

1. In a large saucepan, bring water to a boil and add salt. Stirring constantly, add grits until well incorporated. Reduce heat to medium-low and simmer 35 minutes, stirring constantly. Grits are done when they are soft and creamy.
2. Turn off heat and stir in the cheese and black pepper. Set aside, covered, until the Shrimp Sauce is ready.

Shrimp Sauce

¼ cup vegetable oil
¼ cup chopped yellow onion
¼ cup chopped green bell pepper
¼ cup chopped red bell pepper
3 cloves garlic, minced
2 pounds shrimp, peeled and deveined
¼ cup all-purpose flour
4 cups shrimp stock
2 tablespoons Chef Celeste's Senior Seasonings Creole Garlic, or substitute your favorite Creole seasoning
2 teaspoons cracked black pepper
1 teaspoon salt

1. In a large pot set over medium-high heat, add the oil and sauté onion and bell peppers until tender, about 7 minutes. Add garlic and cook 30 seconds.
2. Add shrimp and coat with flour in the pot. This may sound odd, but it works. Stir in stock, Creole Garlic seasoning, black pepper, and salt. Reduce heat to medium and cook until thickened. Serve shrimp sauce over hot grits.

Seafood Fettuccine

Makes 6 servings

- 1 pound dry fettuccine
- 1 tablespoon salt, plus 2 teaspoons, divided
- 1 quart heavy cream
- ½ pound crawfish tails
- ½ pound shrimp, peeled and deveined
- ¼ pound crab meat
- ½ cup grated Parmesan cheese, plus more for serving
- ½ cup chopped fresh parsley, plus more for serving
- 3 cloves garlic minced
- 2 tablespoons butter
- 1 tablespoon granulated garlic
- 1 tablespoon coarse black pepper
- ¼ teaspoon cayenne pepper

1. Bring a large pot of water and 1 tablespoon salt to a boil. Cook fettuccine until al dente and drain.
2. Combine remaining ingredients, including the 2 teaspoons salt, in a large saucepan. Cook until the sauce has thickened and the shrimp is cooked through.
3. Add the pasta to the sauce. Top each serving with Parmesan and fresh parsley.

Tip: The seafood sauce is also delicious over baked potatoes and fried catfish. To make a great seafood mold, first cook the seafood and set aside to cool. Make the sauce by substituting 6 ounces cream cheese for the heavy cream. Add the cooled seafood to the sauce, pour into an oiled seafood mold, and chill.

Crab Cakes with Chef Celeste's Rémoulade

Makes 4 servings

There are two basic versions of rémoulade sauce—red and white. My sauce is sort of pink and is the best of both worlds.

Chef Celeste's Rémoulade (recipe follows)
1 pound jumbo lump crabmeat
¼ cup small-diced onion
¼ cup small-diced bell pepper
2 tablespoons mayonnaise
2 tablespoons breadcrumbs
2 teaspoons chopped fresh parsley
1 teaspoon granulated garlic
¼ teaspoon salt
¼ teaspoon black pepper
Pinch cayenne
¼ cup olive oil
4 tablespoons (½ stick) soft butter

1. Make Chef Celeste's Rémoulade and refrigerate until ready to serve the crab cakes.
2. Gently combine crabmeat, onion, bell pepper, mayonnaise, breadcrumbs, parsley, granulated garlic, salt, black pepper, and cayenne. Form into 4 patties and chill at least 1 hour.
3. Meanwhile, combine the olive oil and butter. When ready to cook, place a large, heavy-bottomed skillet over medium heat and add the olive oil and butter mixture. When the oil is hot, add the crab cakes. Cook on both sides until golden brown, about 4 minutes each side.
4. Serve crab cakes warm topped with Chef Celeste's Rémoulade.

Chef Celeste's Rémoulade

Makes 1 cup

1 cup mayonnaise
2 teaspoons mustard
2 teaspoons hot sauce
1 teaspoon smoked paprika
1 teaspoon chopped dill pickle
Pinch cayenne pepper

Combine all ingredients and refrigerate until ready to use.

Fried Catfish with Tartar Sauce

Makes 4 servings

4 cups vegetable or peanut oil
4 large catfish fillets, thawed if frozen
½ teaspoon salt
½ teaspoon black pepper
½ teaspoon granulated garlic
½ teaspoon Cajun seasoning
½ cup yellow prepared mustard
For serving: Tartar Sauce (recipe follows)

Cornmeal Seasoning

1 cup yellow cornmeal
½ cup all-purpose flour
2 tablespoons granulated garlic
2 teaspoons Cajun seasoning
1 teaspoon salt
1 teaspoon black pepper
½ teaspoon cayenne pepper

1. Pour oil into a large cast iron or heavy-bottomed skillet set on medium-high heat. Heat oil to 360°F.
2. While oil is heating, rinse catfish and pat dry. In a bowl, combine salt, black pepper, granulated garlic, and Cajun seasoning. Coat fish with mustard, then seasoning mixture. Set fish aside.
3. In a large, shallow bowl, combine all cornmeal seasoning ingredients. When oil is hot, dredge the seasoned fish fillets in the cornmeal mixture, making sure the fish surfaces are completely covered. Fry fish on both sides until golden brown, about 2 minutes on each side. Drain and serve hot with Tartar Sauce.

Tip: For crispy fish chips, cut catfish into thin strips before seasoning them.

Tartar Sauce

Makes 1¼ cups

1 cup mayonnaise
¼ cup chopped dill pickles
1 teaspoon freshly squeezed lemon juice
1 teaspoon sugar
Pinch of salt
Pinch of cayenne pepper (optional)

Combine all ingredients. Cover and refrigerate. Keeps fresh in the refrigerator up to 1 week.

Blackened Catfish

Makes 4 servings

- 4 large catfish fillets, at room temperature
- ¼ cup paprika
- 2 tablespoons granulated garlic
- 1 teaspoon salt
- 1 teaspoon dried basil
- 1 teaspoon dried oregano
- 1 teaspoon dried thyme
- 1 teaspoon black pepper
- ½ teaspoon cayenne pepper
- ¼ cup olive oil
- 1 teaspoon salt
- 4 tablespoons (½ stick) melted butter (optional)
- ¼ cup white wine (optional)

1. Place a large cast iron or heavy-bottomed skillet over high heat. The skillet should be heated until it is extremely hot, almost to the point of smoking.
2. While the skillet is heating, rinse fish and pat dry. In a bowl, combine paprika, garlic, salt, basil, oregano, thyme, black pepper, and cayenne.
3. When ready to cook, coat fish with oil, then season liberally with seasoning mixture. Sear fish on both sides, about 3 minutes each side, then reduce heat and continue to cook for 5 minutes. To make optional sauce, combine melted butter and wine. Pour over plated fish.

Seafood Gumbo

Makes 10 servings

Filé is made from dried, ground sassafras leaves and is used to thicken and flavor gumbo. This seasoning powder was introduced to the early Creoles by the Choctaws. It's not something I grew up eating, but I quickly learned about it when I arrived on the Louisiana culinary scene.

1 pound sliced okra
Salt and pepper to taste
2 pounds smoked pork sausage, diced (optional)
1 large onion, chopped
1 large green bell pepper, chopped
2 ribs celery, chopped
½ cup vegetable oil
½ cup all-purpose flour
8 cups water or chicken stock
2 pounds peeled and deveined shrimp
1 pound lump crab meat
4 gumbo crabs quartered
3 cloves garlic, minced
1 bay leaf
For serving: hot cooked rice, chopped green onion, and filé powder

1. Preheat oven to 350°F. On a cookie sheet, spread okra and sprinkle with salt and pepper to taste. Roast until slightly browned, about 20 minutes, or until it does not appear slimy when stirred. Set aside.
2. In a large Dutch oven set over medium-high heat, sauté sausage, onion, bell pepper, and celery until brown. Remove mixture from pot and set aside.
3. To make a roux, add the oil and flour to the pot and cook over medium-high. Stirring constantly with a wooden spoon, cook until roux is the color of a dark chocolate bar. If roux does burn, let it cool, throw it away, and start over.
4. Add the water, shrimp, crab meat, gumbo crabs, garlic, bay leaf, and salt and pepper to taste. Stir in the reserved cooked sausage and okra. Cover the pot and bring mixture to a boil. Turn the heat to low and simmer 30 minutes.
5. Serve gumbo hot, ladled into individual serving bowls. Scoop cooked rice on top of each serving. Garnish each bowl with a pinch of green onion and a sprinkling of filé.

Marinated Crab Claws

Makes 4 servings (begin a day ahead)

This easy recipe is one of the Chef Celeste LLC catering go-tos. I love the idea of making something flavorful and versatile that comes together fast, which gives me time to work on my other catering tasks. One day I got creative and made a circle of seasoned soft cream cheese in the middle of a platter. I then fanned these crab claws in a double circle around the cream cheese and poured marinade on top of everything. It was beautiful and delicious.

2 pounds crab claws
½ cup olive oil
½ cup white vinegar
½ cup chopped red onion
2 cloves roasted garlic, mashed
3 tablespoons sugar
2 teaspoons chopped fresh parsley
1 teaspoon cayenne pepper
1 teaspoon cracked black pepper
¼ teaspoon salt
For serving: shaved Parmesan cheese (optional)

Combine all ingredients and refrigerate overnight. Serve cold or hot.

5

Beef

At twenty-two years old, I married the love of my life—or so I thought. Actually, by the day of the wedding, I no longer wanted any part of it. Long story short, I stayed married one year, joined the National Guard, and started my career as an MP, a military police officer. This move led me to Alabama and subsequently to Hawaii, where on the military base I worked as a cosmetologist. I eventually had to change my Military Occupational Specialty (MOS) to a cook because the National Guard did not have any military police slots available.

While still stationed in Hawaii, I was allowed to join the mess section because a couple of sergeants didn't want to go to annual training. That's where I learned to cook in large batches, which was actually not difficult. Large-batch cooking is just math; multiply the ingredients in the recipe.

The beef dish I will never forget is Prime Rib Steamship Round. These huge bone-in cuts weighed 80–100 pounds. They were great for presentation and easy carving. While out in the field for one of our two-week annual training sessions, I came up with one of my most creative dishes. We had cases of apples that would have gone to waste, so off the top of my head I made a big pan of stewed apples. My recipe was a huge hit.

Kitchens back then were male-dominated. Cooking with only men was at times a bit challenging. Women were not considered as professionally competent, which perplexed me. I always thought, Don't moms do most of the cooking at home? Haven't most people learned to cook from a woman?

At first, my male kitchen counterparts did not show me respect. In little time, however, I earned it. I feel male chefs still do not show female counterparts the respect they truly deserve, but women chefs are making headway.

After the military I took my career in another direction and enrolled in school at Leeward Community College in Waipahu for speech therapy. On a whim, I took a leisure baking class. I ended up studying the culinary arts for eighteen months, which rekindled my insatiable love for cooking.

Standing Rib Roast

Makes 12 servings

If you are not cooking for a crowd, you can easily halve this recipe. Cooking time will be shorter.

One 6- to 7-rib standing rib roast, at room temperature
1 tablespoon salt
1 teaspoon ground black pepper
1 cup minced fresh herbs
4 cloves garlic, smashed
1 tablespoon extra-virgin olive oil
2 teaspoons smoked paprika

1. Preheat oven to 450°F. Thoroughly season meat with salt and pepper. Make a seasoning paste by combining the herbs, garlic, olive oil, and paprika. Rub all over the meat.

2. Place meat bone-side down in a roasting pan or on a sheet pan. Roast 20 minutes in the hot oven. Turn heat down to 350°F and continue to roast until the meat registers 115°F in the center for rare or 125°F for medium-rare. (The roast will continue to cook after you remove it from the oven. Start checking the temperature after an hour. Depending on roast size and uncooked temperature, cooking could take 1½ hours or longer.)

3. Remove from oven. Before carving, cover meat with foil and let rest at room temperature for 20 minutes.

Pot Roast

Makes 8 servings (begin a day ahead)

The key to this recipe's great brown gravy is to sear the meat well. The caramelization adds color and flavor, so don't skip this step.

2-pound chuck roast
2 tablespoons dry steak seasoning
2 tablespoons Chef Celeste's Creole Garlic Seasoning, or equal parts Italian seasoning, paprika, and onion powder
¼ cup vegetable oil
4 cups water
1 cup red wine
8 new potatoes, quartered
1 yellow onion, chopped
1 medium bell pepper, chopped
1 medium carrot, sliced
6 cloves crushed garlic
1 bay leaf
2 tablespoons all-purpose flour (optional)

1. Coat meat with steak seasoning and Creole Garlic Seasoning. Cover and refrigerate overnight.

2. When ready to cook, preheat oven to 375°F. In a Dutch oven or large heavy pot, heat oil on high and sear meat well all over. This can take 30 minutes.

3. Add remaining ingredients and bake, covered, for 3 hours. The meat should be fork-tender by then.

4. To thicken the jus (pan juices) mash a few vegetables and potatoes around the meat in the pan. To make it thicker, gently stir in a few table-spoons of flour slurry, a mixture of equal parts flour and water. Bake the roast, uncovered, an additional 20 minutes.

5. Remove the meat from the pan and let it rest 5 minutes. Bring the gravy in the pan to a quick boil and check the consistency and seasoning. Slice the meat and return to the pan. Serve meat and gravy warm.

Seared Beef Tenderloin with Compound Butter Sauce

Makes 4 servings

The is one of my favorite go-to recipes for dinner parties. It pairs extremely well with red wine.

3 tablespoons olive oil
4 (8-ounce) beef tenderloins
2 tablespoons dry steak seasoning
1 sweet onion, julienned
6 cloves garlic, minced
1 cup red wine
2 tablespoons salted butter

1. Over high heat, add oil to a large cast iron skillet and heat until very hot. Sprinkle the steaks with the steak seasoning and sear them well on both sides.

2. Reduce heat to medium and add onion and garlic. Cook the steak to medium-rare, 7 minutes on both sides, or until the internal temperature reaches 125°F. Remove the steaks to a warm platter. Stir in the wine and butter and reduce by half.

3. Place the steaks back in the pan and coat with the sauce. Serve immediately.

Tenderloin Tail Kabobs

Makes 8 servings

The tenderloin tail is the smaller end of the tenderloin. It's usually not seen in the average meat market, so ask the butcher to cut them for you. They are so delicious and tender.

2 pounds beef tenderloin tails, cut into 1-inch pieces
¼ cup vegetable oil
½ teaspoon salt
½ teaspoon black pepper
8 (6-inch) metal or wood skewers
1 large red onion, cut into 1-inch pieces
2 cups cherry tomatoes
2 medium zucchini, cut into 1-inch pieces

1. In a large glass bowl, combine beef pieces, vegetable oil, salt, and pepper. Marinate in the refrigerator for at least one hour or, preferably, overnight.
2. When ready to bake, preheat oven to 375°F. On the skewers alternate meat, onion, tomato, and zucchini. For medium-cooked beef, my favorite way of serving this dish, bake 20 minutes. Serve warm.

Honey Sesame Ribs

Makes 5 servings

1 rack ribs, your favorite kind of meat (I recently tried wild boar ribs . . . yum.)
¼ cup granulated garlic
¼ cup sugar
¼ cup chili powder
¼ cup dry steak seasoning
2 teaspoons salt
½ cup honey
3 tablespoons sesame seeds

1. Preheat oven or grill to 300°F. Remove excess fat from ribs. In a bowl, combine granulated garlic, sugar, chili powder, steak seasoning, and salt. Rub the seasoning mixture into the meat. Bake on a cookie sheet or over indirect grill heat, covered, for 2 hours.

2. Remove ribs from the heat and cut into individual pieces. Coat pieces with honey and sprinkle with sesame seeds. Bake, uncovered, 20 additional minutes. For grilling, put honey-coated ribs in a fire-safe pan or on a sheet of foil.

Veal Normandy

Makes 4 servings

This simple classic dish originated in the nineteenth century in Normandy, France, a region famous for its dairy products.

3 tablespoons butter, divided
4 (4-ounce) slices baby veal leg, tenderized
¼ teaspoon each salt, ground black pepper, and granulated garlic
2 cups all-purpose flour
2 tablespoons cracked black pepper
4 ounces wild mushrooms, rehydrated with water and port, then diced
1 ounce cognac
2 tablespoons demi-glace, or a mixture of equal parts brown gravy, beef broth, and red wine
¼ cup heavy cream
Salt and pepper to taste

1. In a large, heavy-bottomed skillet, melt 2 tablespoons butter over medium heat. Season the veal with salt, pepper, and granulated garlic.

2. Dredge the veal slices in the flour and shake off the excess. Cook in the hot butter on both sides until the veal is nicely browned, about 6 minutes each side.

3. Remove the veal to a warm platter. Discard the butter but do not wash the pan. In the same pan, add cracked black pepper and the mushrooms. Add the cognac, and when it is hot, carefully light it with a match.

4. When the flame goes out, add the demi-glace. Swirl to mix and add the cream and remaining tablespoon butter. Bring to a boil and add the veal slices, heating to just warm them up. Serve immediately.

Grits and Grillades

Makes 4 servings

Grillades are pieces of tenderized beef served with a flavorful, hearty gravy. It's a traditional Creole food that originated in New Orleans and is commonly served for breakfast. It can be found on many menus for Queen's balls during the Mardi Gras Carnival season.

¼ cup vegetable oil
2 pounds cubed top round or top sirloin beef steak
⅓ cup all-purpose flour
3 tablespoons Cajun seasoning
1 teaspoon ground black pepper
1 large onion, diced
½ cup diced green bell pepper
½ cup diced red bell pepper
3 tablespoons minced garlic
2 cups beef broth
1 cup chopped ripe tomatoes
1 bay leaf
1 teaspoon hot sauce
1½ teaspoons Worcestershire sauce
1½ teaspoons red wine
For serving: Grits (recipe page 47)

1. Add oil to a large, heavy skillet set over medium heat. While oil is heating, pat beef pieces dry with paper towels. In a bowl, combine flour, Cajun seasoning, and black pepper. Coat steaks with the flour mixture.
2. Brown meat on both sides in hot oil, about 2 minutes per side. Add onion, bell peppers, and garlic and simmer 20 minutes.
3. Add broth, tomatoes, bay leaf, hot sauce, Worcestershire, and wine and bring to a simmer. Cook until sauce is thickened, about 15 minutes.
4. Place a cup or so of hot grits in the middle of 4 serving plates. Top grits with hot grillades and vegetable sauce and serve.

6

Vegetables & Sides

My first actual paid cooking job was in Hawaii at the Salvation Army Alcohol Treatment Center. I was the first female chef they ever hired. The Salvation Army had been reluctant to hire women because of the nature of the job.

While there, I served recently released male inmates who were taking that first step toward reintegration into society. I did so on weekends and without direct supervision. I quickly figured out that these men were focused on returning home and had little personal interest in my presence. Looking back on this experience, I now realize where my passion for training incarcerated men comes from. As we worked side-by-side in the kitchen, I saw in them the drive to succeed—not to mention the respectful acceptance of a female in charge of the kitchen. This experience, probably more than any, prompted me to enroll in Leeward Community College in Hawaii, where I graduated with a degree in food science.

Today, I find joy in teaching local inmates to cook. I also find great happiness when shopping at Baton Rouge's Red Stick Farmers' Market, which offers the freshest produce available. Several times a week, vendors come from miles around to sell to jam-packed crowds that jostle to score the best of whatever is in season.

I hosted cooking demonstrations for eight years at the market, and I have gotten to know many local farmers. I tip my hat to their tireless dedication to growing fruits and vegetables, which are the cornerstone of any well-balanced meal.

Growing up in Detroit, we had a small garden with greens, green beans, herbs, and muscadines. My father loved to make wine, even though neither he nor my mother drank. Today I use his wine-making crock as an end table in my living room.

White Beans / Red Beans and Rice

Makes 8 servings (begin a day ahead)

I first began cooking beans and rice when I was invited to participate in Red Beans and Rice Mondays, a local event started by jazz musician Michael Foster. This event raises money to purchase keyboards for public schools. Each week we provide identical ingredients to local chefs, and they put their own spin on the dish. The results are delicious and different each time. You, too, can take this recipe and make it your own.

- 2 pounds dry white navy beans *or* dry red kidney beans
- 3 tablespoons vegetable oil
- 1 medium yellow onion, chopped
- 1 bell pepper, chopped
- 1 stalk celery, chopped
- 4 cloves garlic, minced
- 3 quarts water or salt-free chicken broth
- 1 smoked turkey leg
- 1 tablespoon salt
- 1 tablespoon cracked black pepper
- 1 tablespoon granulated garlic
- 1 teaspoon dried thyme
- For serving: hot cooked rice and cornbread, sliced pork sausage (optional)

1. Rinse the beans and place them in a large bowl. Add enough water to top the beans by 2 inches and soak the beans overnight.

2. The next day, drain the beans. Place a large stockpot over medium-high heat and add the oil. When the oil is hot, add the onion, bell pepper, celery, and garlic and sauté 3 minutes. Add beans and remaining ingredients and bring to a boil. Cook 30 minutes.

3. Reduce heat to a gentle simmer and cook 2 hours, stirring often. Once the beans are tender, smash a few against the side of the pot to thicken. Serve the beans over rice with a side of hot cornbread. Add sliced pork sausage if desired.

Tip: Combine all ingredients in a crock pot and let it cook while you're at work. (This takes 8 hours on low heat.)

Garlic-Herb Lima Beans

Makes 6 servings

1 pound large fresh lima beans
2 tablespoons olive oil
1 medium onion, chopped
½ cup chopped bell pepper
6 cups water
2 tablespoons roasted garlic
2 tablespoons Chef Celeste's Creole Garlic Seasoning, or equal parts Italian seasoning, paprika, and onion powder
1 tablespoon chopped fresh parsley
1 teaspoon salt
1 teaspoon black pepper

1. Clean the lima beans well and rinse with cold water to remove dirt and any rocks. Add oil to a stockpot set over medium heat and sauté the onion and bell pepper 3 minutes. Add remaining ingredients, bring to a boil, and cook 20 minutes.
2. Reduce to a simmer, cover, and cook until beans are tender, about 1 hour. Remove from heat and serve warm.

Tip: You can blend the cooked beans and serve as a dip with chips. Or add bean broth to blended beans and serve as a soup.

Brown Rice Pilaf

Makes 8 servings

This is good with kabobs.

3 cups chicken broth
1 cup water
2 cups uncooked brown rice
¼ cup chopped onion
¼ cup chopped green onion
½ teaspoon salt
1 pinch chopped fresh parsley

1. In a large saucepan, bring broth and water to a boil. Stir in rice. Reduce heat to a bare simmer. Cover the pot and cook until rice is tender, about 25 minutes.
2. Stir in onion, green onion, salt, and parsley. Turn off the heat, cover the pot, and let sit 5 minutes. When ready to serve, fluff with a fork.

Tip: Water can replace the broth.

Orange Zest Cranberry Sauce

Makes 2 cups

This tastes great over vanilla ice cream, pound cake, or biscuits.

1 pound fresh cranberries
2 cups water
1½ cups sugar
1 cup white wine
1 tablespoon orange zest

1. Combine all the ingredients in a saucepan and bring to a boil. Once everything is nice and bubbly, turn the heat down to a simmer. Cook, uncovered, until reduced by half, about 30 minutes.
2. Remove the sauce from the heat and let it cool. Refrigerate up to 2 weeks.

Easy Pico de Gallo

Makes 2 cups (make a day ahead)

2 tomatoes, diced
2 bell peppers, chopped
½ medium onion, diced
¼ cup chopped parsley
2 garlic cloves, minced
Juice from 1 lemon
½ teaspoon coarsely ground black pepper
1 pinch salt

Combine all ingredients and refrigerate overnight.

7

Desserts

When I left Hawaii behind, my culinary journey took me to Lorton, Virginia, where I joined the team at Sunrise Senior Living Complexes. My duties at this retirement home included providing senior residents with nutritional and quality meals. I wrote menus, procured staples, and managed the dietary staff of four. My responsibilities came to include traveling to various senior complexes in the area and staging special events for seniors.

This experience set me on my career path of upgrading senior dining with delicious and nutritious meals. It was my work at Sunrise that gave me the courage to eventually create and market my proprietary Senior Seasoning blends. This job also unintentionally trained me to be a business manager. I vividly recall an incident during my training when a coworker candidly expressed doubt about my longevity in the industry, due to my inherently kind nature. Oh, how times have changed.

While in Virginia, I also catered for a few Pentagon departments. For one function I peeled and prepared eight hundred deviled eggs. (Never again!) It was during this time that I honed my skills as a professional chef and culinary entrepreneur.

In 1996 I moved with my family from Virginia to Louisiana. I immediately applied for positions at local bakeries, but to no avail. I wanted to work in bakeries because in my teen years I had baked cakes for friends' birthday celebrations. At that time I also enjoyed styling hair, and I never imagined that I would become a chef. Since my first love was hairstyling, I dreamed of having a salon with an adjacent restaurant that would pamper my clientele. Today, that is called a spa retreat. (The mind of a child!)

Finally, Gambino's, a popular bakery chain, hired me, I think because my handwriting was pretty and would look good on cakes. I worked there for a year or so, baking and decorating birthday cakes and cookies and learning the bakery business. To gain more experience, during this time I also volunteered in the restaurant of my newfound friend Ron Sonnier. Without a doubt, my early years in Louisiana were my unofficial apprenticeship in mastering Creole and Cajun cuisine.

Bread Pudding with Vanilla Sauce

Makes 12 servings

Louisiana bread pudding is very different from versions prepared in northern states. Ours is more pudding-like and we almost always top it with a sweet sauce. New Orleans bread pudding sauces are typically made with bourbon or rum.

4 (medium-size) loaves day-old French bread
2 quarts whole milk
4 cups sugar
6 large eggs
2 tablespoons vanilla extract, or the seeds scraped from 2 vanilla beans
For serving: Vanilla Sauce (recipe follows)

1. Preheat oven to 375°F. In a large bowl, break bread into 2-inch chunks. In another large bowl, whisk together the milk, sugar, eggs, and vanilla. Stir in the bread and transfer to a 9×13 buttered, deep baking dish.
2. Bake until doubled in size and golden brown, about 40 minutes. Serve warm topped with Vanilla Sauce.

Vanilla Sauce

Makes 3½ cups

3 cups heavy cream
2 cups sugar
2 tablespoons butter
1 tablespoon vanilla extract

1. Combine all ingredients in a heavy-bottomed saucepan set over medium-high heat. Stir constantly for 15 minutes.
2. Reduce heat to low and cook an additional 5 minutes, stirring constantly. Once the sauce coats the back of a spoon, it's ready.

Easy Pralines

Makes 10 large or 20 small candies

Before I had ever made my first batch of pralines, I was hired to make five hundred pieces for a wedding. Eagerly, I said yes. Then the work began, and my lack of praline-making experience was exposed. (I quickly learned not to volunteer so eagerly.)

This particular recipe is a quick and easy way of making Louisiana's famous candy. Since I have been using it, I'm not hesitant to make pralines. Working quickly is the key to making any praline recipe a success. Don't fret if it takes multiple attempts to get it just right. Eat your mistakes—they will still taste great!

2 cups sweetened condensed milk
¼ cup granulated sugar
3 tablespoons butter, divided
1 pound pecan halves or pieces
1 teaspoon vanilla extract

1. Lay a sheet of wax paper or aluminum foil on a hard work surface. Combine condensed milk, sugar, and 1 tablespoon butter in a heavy-bottomed saucepan. Stirring constantly with a wooden spoon, bring to a boil and cook 10 minutes. Reduce to a simmer and cook and stir until thickened, about 2 more minutes. Stir in the pecans and continue stirring until semi-hardened.

2. Remove from heat and stir in remaining 2 tablespoons butter and vanilla. Immediately drop candies on wax paper using a 2-teaspoon scoop or a scant tablespoon. Cool until firm. Store covered at room temperature.

Tip: You can add chocolate chips to the hot praline mixture. You can also substitute coconut milk for the condensed milk.

Pâte à Choux Puffs

Makes about 24

These puffy pastries are the base for filled cream puffs and eclairs. They are also delicious on their own.

1 cup water
4 ounces (1 stick) butter
1 pinch salt
6 ounces (1¼ cups) all-purpose flour
½ pound eggs (approximately 4 large eggs), unbeaten
1 teaspoon sugar, optional

1. Heat oven to 400°F. Combine water, butter, and salt in a saucepan. Bring to a boil and cook until butter is completely dissolved. Stir in the flour and stir quickly and constantly until the mixture does not stick to the sides of the pan, about 1 minute.

2. Remove pan from heat. Let cool 5 minutes, stirring occasionally. Transfer to a large bowl. Mixing at medium speed, add eggs one at a time, beating between additions. After all eggs are incorporated, beat until the mixture is smooth and shiny, about 2 minutes.

3. Transfer batter to a pastry bag with a tip suited for the size and shape you need for the puffs you want. On a sheet pan lined with parchment, pipe out scant ¼-cup balls of dough 3 inches apart for standard-sized puffs. Bake 15 minutes at 400°F, then reduce to 350°F for another 15 minutes. Before taking puffs out of the oven, make sure they are light and firm, or they will collapse.

Sweet Potato Pie

Makes 2 (8-inch) pies

4 large sweet potatoes, baked and peeled
1 cup sweetened condensed milk
¼ cup evaporated milk
1 large egg
¼ cup brown sugar
1 teaspoon vanilla extract
2 (8-inch) deep-dish pie shells, unbaked

1. Preheat oven to 375°F. Add baked sweet potatoes to a blender or food processor and process on medium speed until smooth. Turn blender to low and completely blend in condensed milk, evaporated milk, egg, brown sugar, and vanilla. Divide filling between the 2 pie shells. Wrap strips of aluminum foil around the edges of the pie shells to prevent over-browning.
2. Bake pies 30 minutes. Rotate them, remove foil from pans, and bake an additional 20 minutes. Remove from oven and cool thoroughly. Pies set as they cool.

Tip: I prefer my pies on the dry side, but if you want a less dense pie, reduce the cooking time by 10 minutes. For a nondairy pie, use sweetened condensed coconut milk instead of condensed milk, and almond milk instead of evaporated milk.

King Cake

Makes 10 servings

Cake

2 cups all-purpose flour
2 tablespoons sugar
2 tablespoons fast-acting yeast
¾ teaspoon salt
1 cup whole milk
2 tablespoons (¼ stick) butter
1 large egg, slightly beaten
½ teaspoon vegetable oil

Filling

½ cup granulated sugar
2 tablespoons cinnamon

Icing

2 cups powdered sugar
2 teaspoons milk
Purple, green, and gold dusting sugar

1. To make Cake, in a large mixing bowl, combine flour, sugar, yeast, and salt. In a small saucepan, gently heat milk and butter to 110°F. Remove pan from heat and whisk in the egg. Pour the milk mixture into the center of the flour mixture and thoroughly blend with your hands.
2. Coat your hands with the vegetable oil and knead the dough on a hard surface 3 minutes. Roll the dough into a ball and place it in an oiled bowl. Cover with plastic wrap and let sit in a warm, draft-free area 20 minutes.
3. Cut dough in half and roll each half into 3×7 pieces. To make Filling, combine the granulated sugar and cinnamon. Sprinkle half of filling mixture evenly on top of each piece of rolled dough. Beginning from the long ends, roll each dough half into a log. Twist or pinch the ends of the logs together to form one large oval.

4. Lightly oil a large baking sheet. Place the cake on the sheet and cover lightly with a cloth. Place the cake back into the warm, draft-free area for another 20 minutes.

5. While cake is rising, preheat oven to 350°F. Bake the cake until golden brown, about 40 minutes. Cool 5 minutes in the pan, then remove to a cooling rack. When completely cool, make Icing by combining the powdered sugar and milk. Spread the icing on top of the cooled cake, then sprinkle liberally with dusting sugar, making 2-inch alternate bands of the individual colors.

Chef French's Famous Brownies

Makes 12 servings

The late Jean French was a classically trained French chef who worked in Baton Rouge restaurants, taught at the Baton Rouge Community College, and ended his career by helping with Meals on Wheels. Chef French was a mentor to me, as well as many other chefs in the Baton Rouge area.

6 tablespoons (¾ stick) butter
6 ounces semisweet chocolate
2 cups sugar
2½ teaspoons vanilla extract
6 large eggs
1½ cups sifted all-purpose flour
1½ cups chopped pecans

1. Preheat oven to 325°F. Generously oil the insides of a 9×13-inch baking pan and set aside. In a saucepan set over low heat, melt together the butter and chocolate until smooth. Remove mixture a large bowl.
2. Add sugar and use a spoon to mix until smooth. Add vanilla, then eggs one by one, mixing well between additions and stirring until smooth. Add flour and pecans and mix well.
3. Pour batter into the prepared pan and bake until a toothpick comes out clean ¾ of the way from the top of the toothpick, about 35 to 40 minutes. It's okay if the bottom of the toothpick is a little dirty; you don't want to overcook the brownies, or they will be dry. Remove from oven and cool before cutting into squares.

Tip: For a holiday treat, add pitted cherries to the batter.

8

Lagniappe

(Something Extra)

With senior dining still my focus, I eventually took a job at a retirement home in Baton Rouge called the Retirement Center. A year later I received a call to help open a new senior complex from the ground up, Lake Sherwood Village.

Lake Sherwood was a beautiful concept and building, where seniors dined restaurant-style, ordering from the table while gazing out on the beautiful lake. I was the food service director in charge of all dining experiences. We provided breakfast and lunch. Residents could eat in the dining room or order room service. At the time, this was my only job; I had not yet started any catering or restaurants.

I vividly recall my dad flying in from Detroit to visit and tour the Lake Sherwood Village building. My father was always my biggest cheerleader. (As a child during the 1970s I loved to watch television, and he would say that I was going to make $30,000 with my own show on television. Guess who now has a television show?) Unfortunately, pancreatic cancer took my father away much too soon. My work at Lake Sherwood Village was one of the few of my accomplishments he lived to see.

When I lived at my childhood home, I often fried eggs for my dad. One of my good friends still talks about my perfectly cooked over-easy eggs. I used a simple technique of having the pan hot, adding the oil, then cracking in the egg. Flip as soon as the white is cooked, and there you have it.

This same friend often advised me to place a book in front of myself to conceal my daydreaming tendencies. Back in Detroit, I would often try to imagine my life in the future. Those fantasies were deeply rooted in the belief that your daydreaming thoughts can subtly steer you toward the very outcomes you imagine, whether advantageous or otherwise.

French Toast

Makes 4 servings

1 cup whole milk
2 large eggs
½ cup granulated sugar
1 teaspoon vanilla extract
8 tablespoons (1 stick) butter
4 thick slices bread
For serving: powdered sugar and syrup

1. In a bowl, combine milk, eggs, granulated sugar, and vanilla. Place a large skillet over medium-high heat and melt the butter. Dip the bread in the milk mixture, taking care not to leave it in too long, or you'll make it soggy.

2. Cook the bread slices in the hot butter until golden brown, 3–5 minutes on each side. Place on plates and sift with powdered sugar. Drizzle on a little syrup and serve hot.

Tapenade

Makes 4 servings

1 pint pitted kalamata olives
4 garlic cloves
¼ cup olive oil
1 ounce anchovies
3 tablespoons freshly squeezed lemon juice
2 tablespoons capers
1 teaspoon fresh thyme
1 teaspoon fresh oregano

Add all ingredients to the bowl of a food processor. Use the pulse button to process to a rough chop. Refrigerate until ready to serve.

Marinade for Smoked Duck and Chicken

Makes about 3 cups

2 cups olive oil
⅔ cup red wine vinegar
4 tablespoons soy sauce
2 tablespoons crushed red pepper
2 tablespoons sesame oil
2 tablespoons tarragon leaves
1½ tablespoons garlic
1 tablespoon salt

Combine all ingredients and use as needed to marinate duck or chicken before smoking them. Marinate your poultry choice at least 2 hours and up to overnight.

Marinade for Shrimp or Seafood

Makes 3 cups

Lemon juice will "cook" raw seafood, so it's best not to marinate fish or shrimp longer than 1 hour.

4 medium green bell peppers, finely chopped
2 medium red bell peppers, finely chopped
2 medium yellow onions, finely chopped
1 stalk celery, finely chopped
2 tablespoons chopped garlic
½ cup red wine vinegar
½ cup olive oil
½ cup freshly squeezed lemon juice
2 tablespoons soy sauce
1 tablespoon sesame oil
½ cup sugar
3½ tablespoons salt
1 tablespoon white pepper
1 tablespoon tarragon
1 tablespoon basil
2 teaspoons oregano
1½ teaspoons cracked fennel
¼ teaspoon cayenne

Combine all ingredients together and use as needed.

Easy Eggs Benedict

Makes 2 servings

You can make this dish extra fancy by topping it with ham, crisp bacon, or sauteed shrimp.

Hollandaise Sauce

2 cups water
1 tablespoon vinegar
4 egg yolks (reserve egg whites for another use)
¼ teaspoon crushed red pepper
1 pinch salt
1 pinch cracked black pepper
1 shake hot sauce
¼ cup (½ stick) melted butter
4 large eggs
2 English muffins, each split in half horizontally
¼ cup fresh spinach leaves

1. To cook the Hollandaise Sauce, in a saucepan, bring the 2 cups water and vinegar to a boil. In a large metal bowl that will fit on top of the saucepan, add egg yolks, red pepper, salt, black pepper, and hot sauce. Place the bowl over the simmering water and whisk with one hand while drizzling in butter with the other. Whisk constantly or the yolks will scramble. (It's easier than it sounds.) When done, the sauce should be light yellow and fluffy and thick enough to coat the back of a spoon. Should take 4–5 minutes. Set aside and keep warm.

2. To make the eggs, crack the 4 eggs and gently drop them in the simmering pot of water and vinegar. Cook until the whites are done but the yolk is still soft, about 6 minutes.

3. While the eggs are poaching, toast the English muffins. Divide between 2 serving plates with split sides up. Top each half with a poached egg and fresh spinach. Pour on the Hollandaise and serve immediately.

Oven Baked Pork Ribs

Makes 3 servings

1 (2½- to 3-pound) slab of pork baby back ribs
2 tablespoons granulated garlic
2 tablespoons Cajun seasoning
¼ teaspoon salt
¼ cup light brown sugar
3 tablespoons apple cider vinegar
½ tablespoon chili powder

1. Preheat oven to 350°F. Trim the fat from the rib slab and set it aside. Combine granulated garlic, Cajun seasoning, and salt, and rub all over the meat.

2. Place the ribs in a baking pan and bake, uncovered, 40 minutes. While ribs are baking, in a bowl combine the brown sugar, vinegar, and chili powder and set aside.

3. Remove the ribs from the oven and top with brown sugar mixture. Cover the pan with aluminum foil. Reduce oven temperature to 325°F and bake an additional 90 minutes. When ready to serve, drizzle with honey and sprinkle with sesame seeds if desired.

Roux 101

Roux is a thickener used to make gravies and gumbo. Even though I was raised up north in Detroit, I have been making Cajun roux since I was a teenager, courtesy of Mr. Justin Wilson, whom I would watch on public television every weekend. Making roux is like second nature to me. Roux is genuinely one of my cherished culinary activities.

Back in Detroit, I would fry chicken or chops and then clean out the pan and make a separate roux for my gravy. Today, I shake my head in disbelief at the thought. Now most of the time I leave the flavorful grease in the pan and use that to make roux.

Many people think it's difficult to make a roux, but it's not. The key is to not rush the process and to constantly stir. If you burn it, you have to start over or the entire dish will taste burnt. When it's your desired color, it's ready to use. Even though there are easy-to-find jars of ready-made roux on grocery shelves, I always make my roux from scratch (though I'm contemplating bottling my roux for sale). If frying, I use the rendered oil from cooking to add depth of flavor.

Here's my recipe:

Use equal parts all-purpose flour and vegetable oil. Whisking constantly, cook in a heavy-bottomed pot over medium heat.

Color Stages of Roux:

White Roux—Since this mixture does not get heated, I really just call this a thickener.

Blond Roux (for white gravies)—While constantly stirring, the roux mixture bubbles around the edges but does not turn colors. Takes about 5 minutes.

Brown Roux (for brown gravies)—Constantly stir and cook the roux mixture until it reaches a medium-brown color.

Dark Roux—This is my favorite roux. Constantly stir until roux mixture reaches a very dark-brown color. At this stage, it's easy to burn, so pay careful attention. Remove from heat as soon as the color is right. I usually transfer this cooked roux to a cooler pot, so that it doesn't continue to cook.

Various shades of roux. At the far right is an example of burned roux. (Photo by author.)

9

Menu Ideas

In 2000, I branched out and opened my own restaurant, Taylor's Old Post Office Café in Baton Rouge. I called my catering company Taylor Made Gourmet Food. At the time, I was remarried and had just given birth to my first child, Taylor.

Our family subsequently expanded through the adoption of siblings Iesha and Ronnie. With the business and the family growing, I was asked to open a restaurant location in a new development that would be a part of revitalizing downtown Baton Rouge, the Red Stick Farmers' Market. This new venture became the location of my restaurant Taylor Made Gourmet, on Fifth Street and Main. I simultaneously opened Cgill's at the corner of Third and North Street. I opened Chef Celeste Bistro inside the farmers' market in 2016 and then, in 2018, my 520 Spain event space in Beauregard Town. I have been a fixture in the downtown Baton Rouge area for twenty-one years now and counting. Downtown Baton Rouge has truly become my domain.

Even with my hectic schedule, I often take time to reflect on my childhood dreams—or what I called nightmares—of food chasing me. I also had bad dreams of a bridge over water in the dark. It's a remarkable irony that today I find myself in Louisiana, a place adorned with bridges and waterways, passionately engaged in the culinary arts. What an extraordinary life mine has shaped into.

Throughout it all, my approach to life and my career revolves around looking for the positive and embracing transformation. While there have been instances where my gender led to oversight and my race resulted in peculiar monikers, my personal mantra has always remained steadfast: "Look out, here I come."

I firmly believe in cultivating confidence in one's abilities and relentlessly pursuing goals. It's life—just enjoy the journey.

Brunch Menu

Shrimp and Grits
French Toast
Scrambled Eggs
Bacon
Sausage
Fresh Fruit
Gourmet Cheese or Charcuterie
Mimosas, Juice, Coffee, Tea

Date Night Menu

Sensation Salad
Shrimp and Corn Soup
Seared Beef Tenderloin with Compound Butter
Garlic Mashed Potatoes
Roasted Asparagus
Bread Pudding with Vanilla Sauce

Buffet Menu

Potato Salad
Seafood Gumbo
Rice
Garden Salad
Fried Catfish with Tartar Sauce
French Bread
Pralines

Tea Party Menu

Cucumber Sandwiches
Open-Faced Chicken Salad Sandwiches
Mini Bread Pudding Bites
Petit Fours
Fruit
Orange Zest Cranberry Sauce
Assorted Teas
Sugar Cubes
Clotted Cream

I actually made this menu for Britcom, an event held by Louisiana Public Broadcasting for British actors, who would fly over from England for a meet and greet.

Recipe Index